How to Start an Online Business from $32 a Month

Start a Web Design Business Blueprint Sell Your Blog and Websites Online

Smit Chacha

Copyright © 2020 Smit Chacha

All rights reserved.

ISBN: 9798679574557

ABOUT THIS BOOK

You will learn how to start an online business from just $32 a month, this is a blueprint in how to start a successful web design business.

Build a WordPress blog from scratch and Sell it Online and start making a living on building and selling blog online.

The business will cost you $32 a month plus electricity and internet cable bills. You will be able to start making a living with this successful online business blueprint.

This is for a novice with a little knowledge of I.T. You will need to know a little bit about how to build WordPress blogs or simply HTML/CSS

This is not a course for absolute beginners. If you do not know how to build WordPress blogs then I suggest you first get a little knowledge of I.T. before starting this blueprint course about how to get successful online.

I will guide you in how to build a professional blog with SEO and Social Media marketing in mind. I will also guide you in how to transform your blog into a paperback and digital book.

And finally, I will tell you how to sell your blog online and make a living out of this web design business.

How to Start an Online Business from $32 a Month

Start a Web Design Business Blueprint Sell Your Blog and Websites Online

We will touch on affiliate marketing and adverting (Amazon, Clickbank and AdSense). I will also touch on Email Marketing and how to start this from $1 a month!

So, without due... let's start this blueprint course!

CONTENTS

How to Start an Online Business from $32 Month 1

How to Choose a Web Hosting Server 9

Finding a Niche to Blog on Regular Bases..12

Keyword Rich Vs Exact Domain Match Domain Name 15

Internet (Static Vs Dynamic) WordPress 18

How to Stand Out as a Brand Online...21

Social Media (Facebook, Twitter, YouTube, Pinterest, etc.)................24

Brands and Keyword 27

Writing Blogposts on Your WordPress Blog 29

Email Marketing and Email Subscribers List.......................................31

Affiliate Marketing...34

Adsense and Google Ads..36

From Blogpost to a Paperback Book 37

Sell Your Website on Flippa.com 39

ABOUT THE AUTHOR..42

ACKNOWLEDGMENTS

I have over 10 years' experience in Web Design, Web Development and Web Marketing. For the past 10 years I have developed several blogs, mobile apps and published several books.

I make a decent living in building WordPress Blogs and Sell them for huge profits and this is what I want to teach you and this blueprint book.

How to Start an Online Business from $32 Month

You are unemployed, no jobs around and you want to start a business. Where can you start with limited capital? If this is what you are seeking then you must read this book.

Here I will guide you in how you can start an online business from just $32 month. If you have this much capital you can turn into a business.

Will that business be successful? Will it turn to hundreds, thousands or even hundreds of thousands? I do not know, only time will tell. However you will have a business that you can work with, in your own time while you search for jobs.

Like any business you need to give time. Running an online business is a little different then running a physical high street shop, how different?

Well to start off a physical high street shop requires you to have merchandise and a place to sell. An online business only requires you to have a website. You do not need to buy any physical merchandise to run an online business. With only $32 a month you can run any successful online business.

How successful is what I cannot guarantee, success depends in how you see your business (what is your vision). If you can get 5 sales of $45 in month while investing only $32 a month that is success. It is profit. Now if you have 1 business that runs like that, imagine having 10 of them or even 20, 30, 40... well you got the idea.

Many people have multiple business while some find success in just 1. Online business is not different in that perspective. If you are satisfied or find success in just 1 business than voila! You do not need to go any further. You know the process in how to turn another $32 in to a successful project.

Any business (online or physical) requires your presence, your time spent. A physical shop will have a certain timetable (when it is in operation or closed). An online business is always open, 24hr a day and worldwide. Your business runs internationally. You can have clients from any part of the world.

You do not need to ship products you can still run a successful business without spending a dime in merchandise. You can run an online business solely based on content where your source of income will come from advertisements or run as an affiliate. You can also dropship products or run it like a physical shop. I will get in detail in later chapters about these.

I just want you to get an idea about what online business is and where to start. If you have $32 you can turn that in to an online business. This is my only point I want to make in this introduction chapter. I hope you will enjoy reading this book and play along on your computer so that by the end of this book you will have your online success!

Note: *For any reason at all, if you cannot find $32 a month or some lump sum amount you can always turn to crowdfunding sources online. Where you ask the people to invest in your vision in your story.*

Now you can ask me, why do I need $32 to start off an online business? Good question. Well if you do not count your house rent, electricity bills, the price of your new computer/laptop, etc. You will need only $32 a month. You will need a hosting server, domain and optionally but recommend an email marketing service.

There are loads on the market, below are what I use and recommend:

Hosting: Hostgator $15/month – you can host unlimited domains or websites.

Domain registration: Godaddy or Namecheap. I recommend that you search online for promotional codes for these, you can save a lot! Typical price for a domain is $10 annum

Email Marketing service: Aweber. Price $49 every 3 months to start off.

As you can see the total amount is around $32 a month. If you want to start off a physical high street shop you will need a lot more than that.

Now that you have a hosting service and a domain to work with, you need to create your first website. I suggest that you install WordPress (a content management system or CMS). WordPress is an open source CMS used by millions of people and business around the world. It is very easy to use.

Domain Name Registration

In this chapter I will show you how to register your first domain name. Choosing the right domain name requires some basic criteria and research.

Your domain is your brand name. This is what your customer will remember, therefore it must be something catchy with the right keywords in mind.

Search Engines such as: Google, Yahoo, Bing and others have ranking criteria that has to match in order for your website or webpages to rank.

Most people will find your website from the search engines. Once your business start to get customers you may find visitors coming to your website directly. It takes time.

Now that you want to start your online business which can be in any niche (health, animals, garments, vehicles, books, etc.). For the purpose of this book we will build a website based on health and fitness niche (weight loss).

Weight loss is a very huge niche, millions of people are looking to lose weight and purchasing merchandise to do so.

To find the right domain name keywords you can use a free tool provide by Google called Google Keyword Planner url:

https://adwords.google.com/KeywordPlanner

In order to use this tool you need to register a free Google Adwords account. It is a very simple process and I do recommend that you read the terms and conditions before accepting it.

Once you are registered and you are under the Google Keyword Planner tool, the below screen will appear:

Once you enter your main keyword, in this case "weight loss" in the field you will find a list of keywords in this niche by clicking on the get ideas button. This works for any given niche.

Once you know your competition you can work with your brand name (domain registration).

Note: You can still rank in the search engines with a brand name that has no keywords in the domain name. However for the purpose of this book I do recommend *that you start off with a domain name that has keywords on the domain so that it is easy to rank on the search engines. Plus it is a good way to market your business online and offline. Keywords on the domain name helps the customer to remember what your business is all about.*

Once you are satisfied on the keywords results it is time to find if that domain name is available for registration. Godaddy also has a domain registration suggestion tool. Just enter your domain name in mind. This process can take some time, but once you found your brand name. Register it and the next step is to find a hosting server.

Web Hosting Server

There are loads of hosting servers in the market. I recommend that you use Hostgator business plan. It costs around $15/month and you can host unlimited domains/websites and unlimited bandwidth.

Once you login to your hosting account you need to add your domain name, you can do that under the CPanel. After that you need to go to your Godaddy account and change the Nameserver details so that your domain is connected to your hosting account.

Every domain that you register on Godaddy or any domain registration service, you are required to change the Nameserver details that matches your Hostgator account (after adding the domain name to your server). This Nameserver details will be same for every domain that you add on.

If you find it difficult in finding your Nameserver details or adding your domain name from CPanel you can always contact Hostgator customer service. They are very friendly staff and they are happy to help you. This is another good reason why I use Hostgator.

How to Choose a Web Hosting Server

When it comes to web hosting there are certain things that you should be aware of, choose a Web server carefully as you do contract with them. Read the fine print and accept their terms and conditions.

Some web host offer 2-way authentication while others don't. This is a good feature to have. It is your security that you should be careful of. Do regular backups you can use Updrafplus WordPress plugin. Keep your backups in a secure folder or hard drive.

Some hosting servers offer huge discounts on 36 months contract, you can save somewhere between £200 to £300. Hostgator is a good example, however it currently offers 2-way authentication.

There are many online review websites for hosting

companies, I recommend that you do a personal research before choosing the right one for your websites. Check the price, Cpanel options, Email options, runtime, etc.

Most webhosts allow to install WordPress from their Cpanel with just one click you will need to change the nameservers on your domain registrar. You will be able to find 2 nameservers on the Cpanel of each webhost. If you find difficulties in finding these technical parts ask the customer service team of your webhost, they should be able to help you with either live chat, email or phone call.

There are many types of webhost: shared hosting, VPN and Private server. Shared hosting packages are the cheapest and if you are an individual that this option will do everything for you. If you are a cooperate company, I would suggest that you go for a Private Server option. These prices range from £250 a month, while shared hosting starts under £5 month and you can save further for a lengthier contract (example mentioned above for Hostgator).

If you do not know PHP/mySQL WordPress makes it easy to create blogposts and websites without coding. WordPress is an open source content management system or CMS. There are others to such as Joomla,

Drupal and others.

WordPress is the most standard one and many large cooperatives and governmental websites use it such as BBC and others. There are many online video tutorials for how to use WordPress on YouTube or you can simply read a book or follow my blog as I will guide you from start to finish in how to succeed in online world (business).

I have published several books on KDP, LULU I have even build several android apps on Google Play Store and I have created and still manage several online blogs made in WordPress.

Finding a Niche to Blog on Regular Bases

If you are thinking to build a blog think of a Niche first this way you know what to write about. Choose a Niche cleverly and be an expert about the topic. Knowing the niche makes easy to write. Blogging is fun when you know how what you are writing about.

You can add advertisement or affiliate products to monetize your blog. Later I will tell you how to get a Google AdSense and many affiliate programs.

A good server is also required I will also guide you how to setup your very first blog using Hostgator server. You will need to setup nameservers on DNS.

You will get that information on your server Cpanel. We

will touch on this is a greater detail in later chapters. But for now, you just need to know that you need a domain, server and WordPress to start blogging.

Finding a Niche to Blog on Regular Bases

A Niche simply means a topic or a title of your blog. All other categories fall over this niche. My niche on this blog is how to succeed online. Find your niche and start writing.

A good way to find a niche is to go Amazon Books categories and find a category that fits your needs or should I say your expertise. Write about that stuff and sooner or later you will have a brilliant online blog with your name on it!

You can also later create an Android App and publish it on Google Play Store or even better publish a book (paperback and digital) on Amazon KDP. I will on later chapters touch in detail about all of these things.

You need a niche for start a blog do not go for multiple niches in just one blog. Do different blogs for each different niche. This way you will have multiple mobile apps and books on your name.

Create Facebook Fan Pages so that your blogs become an online brand. Over time people will start visit your blog and follow you on social media and who knows you might become another successful millionaire online.

Use WordPress to create your blogposts, this CMS (content management system) is Google friendly, meaning the top search engines love to index pages and posts from WordPress blogs. I will later touch in detail about SEO or search engine optimization and how you can rank on the top search results on each popular search engine such as Google.

I will also touch in greater details which plugins you should use on your blog that will boost engagements and popularity of your blogpost.

Keyword Rich Vs Exact Domain Match Domain Name

When it comes to domain names getting an exact match is rare and if you are lucky you can rank very high on major search engines. Keyword rich domain name, simply means that you have certain keywords with or without hyphens and these ones do rank, however are lower class.

Page title matters a lot in terms of ranking, ideally you should fill all the blanks of page meta data and it is 53 characters. Page description is optional as after so many Google updates, page meta description simply vanished.

In terms of images it is a good idea to have ALT tags as these will rank on image searches in major search engines. Social Media such as Pinterest count image hashtags and you should always have them in your account.

Twitter has become out of fashion, nonetheless people still use it. Facebook on the other hand it is a good source of marketing. Having a Facebook Page and sharing your content will boost your ranking and web traffic.

RSS feeds is out to fashion. Slowly social media will also become out of fashion but the good news it that it is still working. If you use it cleverly you can definitely turn your posts into a viral content.

Having a Mailing List is also advisable as you can keep in contact with your readers, however nowadays most mailing lists go to spam folders. Simply ask your readers to add you in their safelist.

Finding the right domain name takes time do your research carefully because this will be the brand name of your blog. It will be hard to change the name of your brand once it is popular.

Plus, once you have a mobile app under your brand it will be harder for people to find you in another name. So, choose a domain name carefully.

There are many domain registrars on the web, the most

popular ones are: Namecheap, GoDaddy and many others. **Tip:** Whenever purchasing a domain name check online for any promo codes, you can save up to 90% on a domain name purchase. I have found GoDaddy promo code for just $0.99 each domain for a year!

My preferred domain registrar in Namecheap but you are free to choose which one you want to go with. Another thing, make sure that you use a 2-way authentication login when you create an account. It is more secure way to maintain a domain registrar account.

Internet (Static Vs Dynamic) WordPress

Computers, internet, search engines, social media is a growing trend. And a trend keeps changing over time. For example you know Facebook and Twitter. When I had a computer at age 11 there was no Facebook or Twitter. Google come afterwards, I used to use Altavista.com (a Yahoo partner) as a search engine.

Presently people are finding Google, Yahoo and Bing the most popular search engines. While Google has the majority of fans, Yahoo and Bing are also trending.

Search engines algorithms has also changed a lot since the beginning of internet. New algorithms are building. If you want to rank on major search engines you must follow and read all the search engines algorithms updates.

Presently and I believe, unique quality content is king. And I believe this trend will continue for many years to come. We all contributed for the success of the internet.

When internet was invented, only a small group of people used it. Nowadays computers are an essential part of everybody homes. Then come the smartphone and things turned mobile.

My websites and blogs receive a ton of mobile traffic every year. Yet I still find websites on search engines that are not mobile friendly. As technology advances we must update to make sure that everybody gets your information.

Static and Dynamic Website

To access any website or blog you need a browser and your browser will only read pure HTML. This is called a static page. Dynamic pages are pages that uses databases and a scripting language to communicate with the server. This book is not about how to build dynamic pages, so I will not go into detail about SQL, databases and scripting language.

WordPress

WordPress is the most common script or software that people use to build dynamic websites or blogs. You just need to install and the software does all the "good stuff" in the background. You do not need to learn any sort of computer programming or scripting language. All the building blocks of building a website is in there.

Other Content Management Systems (CMS)

There are many other CMS such as Joomla, Drupal, etc. Most popular is WordPress and it is very much standard and loved from Google and other major search engines. Feel free to use your preferred one. I use WordPress as a preferred choice.

There are many free and paid plugins and themes in WordPress which you can download and install, you can also edit the code if you know coding. There is also a huge online community that can help you in how to create you own plugins or themes from scratch, just read the documentation for reference.

How to Stand Out as a Brand Online

If you do a simple search of people who stand out in front of the crowd, such as: politicians, musicians, authors, actors, etc. You will notice that their picture and an excerpt of the tiny biography will appear in the search engines side bar.

This means they stand out in front of the crowd. They are a brand, and the process to do this is very simple. You are either a: Politian, musician, author, actor or something else.

Join politics, do your work or start producing music on Apple, or write a book on Amazon KDP. This way you will stand out in front of the crowd and build an online brand.

You will need to proclaim your status with the search

engines as they will automatically add your name and your portfolio in the side bar. Just upload your pictures and you will be famous online.

This is my online success page: **https://g.co/kgs/yVNxZs**

In later chapters I will show you how you can profit even more with your online portfolio.

I will teach you everything here, just keep following my blogposts on regular bases. Following is not enough you should at least do the effort in turning into to a practical tutorial.

By the end on you will have a blog, android app, Facebook Fan Page, social media pages and your very own book in paperback and digital.

I will only touch on android app not on apple apps, the reason why is that android is simpler and cheaper way to publish. You just need to pay a one-time fee of $25 to Google for unlimited apps. While apple you need to have a annual subscription of $99 otherwise you lose your work.

There are many android devices far more than apple. It is true that apple has more apps and you can take android as an advantage for creating new creative apps on Google Play Store.

Subscribe to my mailing list to get latest updates in how to succeed online. It takes time and effort but you will reach there and even further.

Social Media (Facebook, Twitter, YouTube, Pinterest, etc.)

Since the launch of social media websites and platforms marketing become even more easy. Social media platforms such as: Facebook, Twitter, YouTube, Pinterest, Instagram, etc. has revolutionized the online world. These platforms are great to produce and distribute your content. Nowadays it is estimated that people aged 18-65 spend at least 2 hours on social media each day. Teenagers and young adults spend even more time on these platforms. Advertising which once only happened on television, radio and newspapers became more online. Nowadays companies spend more money on online advertising than on television.

It is important to have social media accounts to get

popularity online. You do not need every single one of them. There are so many social media platforms. You just need a few of them and they are: Facebook, Twitter, Instagram, Pinterest, YouTube and that is it.

You need a WordPress blog and on later blogpost I will guide you in how to install one in a webhost. I will also guide you in how to find a web hosting server.

For a blogger you will not need YouTube for a Vlogger YouTube is essential. Anyways it is good to have a YouTube account but it is not necessary.

You can also create an online radio that will be broadcast live but I am not going to touch on that chapter. You can write and publish books or in other words transform your blogpost into a physical book that will be on sale in many online retailers. I will be touching on this in greater detail in later chapters.

Writing is fun and if you love writing you will succeed on the online world. Google and other major search engines love unique content and people also crave for unique written content. Just keep writing and sooner or later you will be popular online.

Social Media and #Hashtage

The best way to go viral on social media is to have

#hastags all over you posts, but not the entire post. Social Media platforms such as Facebook, Twitters, Instagram, Pinterest and others use this common method of hashtags.

A good way to add hashtags is to a complete sentence and the keywords that stand out should be turned into a hashtag, below an example

"A good way to write a #CV or #Resume is to have a maximum of 1 page as many #employers will skip the second page. For more CV writing #tips and #techniques go to LINK and read the following blogpost LINK. Best #employment and #interview getting tips."

As you can see, I have 2 links and my post is embedded with hashtags that are keywords that I want to highlight. These sort of hashtags posts will have better viewing and clicking rates. For Facebook just share on groups that way it is.

Brands and Keyword

To start an online business you need a brand, a name or should I say a domain name. Good quality domain names are short and keyword rich. Meaning something short with your niche keyword in there. These are hard to find as most are already registered. At GoDaddy and other domain registration websites you can do a simple search of your desired domain name and it will tell you if it is available to register, if not they will suggest your variations of the same keyword that are available in the present market.

The reason why you should have a keyword rich domain is for pure SEO basics. We will discuss SEO in later chapters. For now all you need to know is that SEO (search engine optimization) is the mechanics of how internet search marketing works. The more you optimize your online business (the more SEO friendly) the better it will rank online.

Your brand must contain your target keywords for easy SEO. However, you can still rank your websites or blog with totally unique name.

Try to choose a short keyword brand as it is easy to remember. Something without hyphens if you can. Long tailed keywords are easy to rank, however there are fewer searches going on the web.

Have a good 63 characters long page or post title and use your meta description with at least 3 to 4 keywords that you want to rank on the search engines.

You must use your keywords carefully within certain range and I have mentioned above. If you use your keywords carefully you will succeed and get daily, weekly and monthly unique visitors.

You should also install Google Analytics to track your visitors, I will touch in greater detail about how to implement in later chapters.

Subscribe to my mailing list and keep updated with the latest trend in online world.

Writing Blogposts on Your WordPress Blog

Once you have chosen your preferred web host install WordPress with your credentials such as page title, username, email and click on install. You will receive an email with your password which you can change it to whatever you want under the WordPress Dashboard (on user tab).

Change your password and it is recommended that you also change the permalinks to blogpost. It's a good SEO standard to rank pages under this sort of permalinks.

There are many SEO plugins that you can install the most popular is SEO Yoast, easy to install and to create xml sitemaps, which you can submit on Google Webmaster and Bing Webmaster tools. You need an xml sitemap in order to index your pages, posts and websites to Search Engines.

In WordPress there are many free and paid themes that you can choose and activate. Choose a theme and start blogging and writing blogpost. If you have installed SEO Yoast you can set the page title and meta description in order to better rank on Search Engines.

You can add categories, menus and even widgets under those tabs. You can even customize the CSS in most themes, including the free ones. WordPress is very easy to use and fun to publish articles, blogposts, etc.

Tip: There is a Twenty Twelve WordPress Theme which is fully customizable using CSS and there are thousands of online resources in how to create your very own WordPress theme from this one as a child theme.

There are many other open source CMS such as Joomla, Drupal and others. WordPress is the most popular one. Google loves WordPress and ranks them very well.

Email Marketing and Email Subscribers List

A good way to market your products and to make user engagements with your WordPress blog is to have an email subscribers list. Where users can input their name and email address and you can send me daily, weekly, monthly or periodically updates via email.

This way you will have a list of subscribers which you can later on send them newsletters or even physical products based on your blog niche. You will be able to do affiliate marketing via email which you can blast to your followed subscribers and earn hundreds if not thousands of dollars' worth of commissions. This is a common and successfully marketing practice done worldwide with many branded blogs and brands.

You can even launch you own product and market it via email and get people know better your own products. The best way to do email marketing is to make sure that your emails do not go to spam folders. To do that you must let the user have the decency to double opt in to your list.

Meaning they should receive 2 emails once stating that they should confirm your email address and mark as non-spam (safe list). This way you will make sure that they always read your emails and they are not sent to their spam folder and ignored.

There are many email marketing services you can use, such as Aweber.com they charge a monthly fee and gets a bit expensive on the long run.

My advice is to use Sendy by Amazon, you can send 1000 emails for just $1 and there is a limit of 50000 emails per day. Which you can ask to increase later on once you have stablished a huge email list. Just search Sendy Amazon email marketing and you should find the web address or go to **https://sendy.co/**

It is very easy to install on your web server, just follow the guidelines and they have an excellent customer service and a forum where you can ask for help. It cost around $50 and it is a one-time investment. Not a monthly service charge like Aweber and other email marketing services out there.

Affiliate Marketing

A good way to monetarise your blogs is to add affiliate products to your webpages and blogposts. This can come in a variety of ways such as banners, links, etc.

You get a percentage of the product price as a commission and you will be paid directly by the company or affiliate network where you are registered.

There are many affiliate networks out there below are some examples:

- Clickbank.com
- Cj.com (commission junction)
- Markethealth.com
- Sellhepalth.com
- Amazon affiliate program (amazon associates)
- And many more, just do a search on google "affiliate programs" or "affiliate networks" etc

With Amazon affiliate program you can earn up to 4% of each products cost as a form of a commission. The cookie that tracks your affiliate id last only 24 hours, meaning they can purchase any product in 24 hours after being sent to amazon by your affiliate link and you still get a commission. People earn hundreds if not thousands of dollars a month with affiliate products.

And a nice thing about Amazon affiliate links is that they tend to blend very easily and looks good. Just go to **https://affiliate-program.amazon.com/** and open an account and follow the guidelines and you should be good to go.

You can track your affiliate links with a unique affiliate id it is highly recommended that you use at least one id per blog, so you can track and tweak your affiliate links and check your progress.

Amazon pays you every 60 days, meaning for the first payment you will need to wait 60 days and then onwards you should be paid regularly. Just read their terms and conditions, follow their easy to read guidelines and you should be ready to go.

Adsense and Google Ads

Another good way to monetarise your blogs is with Adsense ads by Google. Just go to **https://www.google.com/adsense/start/** and open an Adsense account and start putting Google ads on your blogpost. Your ads will be related to your blogpost and will blend entirely with your blogpost.

You earn a commission per click, meaning every time a user clicks on your Google ads you will get a commission, this can range from $0.01 to $10 solely based on how expensive the ad is. People can make a living based solely on Google Adsense advertisements. They need to write quality and unique content on daily bases to archive that goal.

Again read a follow all Google Adsense guidelines and terms and you should be ready to go.

How to Start an Online Business from $32 a Month

Start a Web Design Business Blueprint Sell Your Blog and Websites Online

From Blogpost to a Paperback Book

Lastly you can transform your blogposts into a physical book where you can royalties based on sales. It is a common practice for many bloggers. They start an online blog and write hundreds of posts and once they are written everything that there is in their niche, they select certain blogposts and transform it into a paperback book.

You can do that on Amazon KDP or via a publisher such as lulu.com

Again, follow the guidelines and you should be ok to go and become a author from a blogger. You will have a Google profile page on the right side with you picture and your books. Whenever people search for your name. Here is an example of mine: search "Smit Chacha" without quotes and you should see my profile picture on Google.

So that it is it, I hope you enjoyed reading this book and for more of my books search on Google, Amazon and other book stores.

Sell Your Website on Flippa.com

Finally, I want to end the chapter and the book with a tip in how to sell your website or blog on flippa.com

Flippa.com is an online platform where people can buy and sell stablished websites and it cost around $49 to insert an adverted. Flippa also charges 10% commission per sale for websites sold under $50k

I have sold multiple blogs and websites on Flippa on an average of $6000 per WordPress blog. u blogs where sold simply because they were getting tons of web organic traffic and revenue.

For example, if your blog gets around 1500 visitors a month and you earn around $200 a month with

Clickbank, Amazon or AdSense you can estimate to your website to be sold at $6000.

People tend to buy websites that are already getting traffic and revenue. An average of 36 months' worth of revenue is what you should aim for. There are sites sold for over 1 million dollars but those websites traffic and revenue is around $50k a month.

It is very easy to sell websites, mobile apps and games on Flippa. It is a simple registration form; you also need to verify your identity by sending a picture of your passport or driving licence. And you can good to go!

You can also buy websites on Flippa and start on online business without the hazzle of starting from scratch. But if you are into web design business than selling your websites on Flippa can give a steady monthly income. I personally make a living on Flippa and Forex.

I start a blog do SEO and social media marketing and start to engage with potential customers, get organic traffic and a few sales and sell it on Flippa. On average I sell 3 to 4 websites on Flippa every 2 years. And generally my blogs get me around $200 per month worth of commissions (affiliate income from Clickbank or Amazon).

So, there you have it! I hope you enjoyed reading this

How to Start an Online Business from $32 a Month

Start a Web Design Business Blueprint Sell Your Blog and Websites Online

book and learn a lot of how to start an online business from just $32 a month!

ABOUT THE AUTHOR

Smit Chacha has been successfully doing online web design business for over 10 years. Her has built a number of websites from scratch, including mobile apps and published several books.

He is a successful businessman, doing web design business online, Forex and book publishing.

www.ingramcontent.com/pod-product-compliance
Lightning Source LLC
Chambersburg PA
CBHW050314220526
45465CB00005B/1990